Hinduism

Sue Penney

Heinemann Library
Chicago, Illinois

© 2001 Reed Educational & Professional Publishing
Published by Heinemann Library,
an imprint of Reed Educational & Professional Publishing,
Chicago, IL

Customer Service 888-454-2279
Visit our website at www.heinemannlibrary.com

Designed by Ken Vail Graphic Design, Cambridge
Originated by Universal
Printed by Wing King Tong in Hong Kong.

05 04 03 02 01
10 9 8 7 6 5 4 3 2

Library of Congress Cataloging-in-Publication Data
Penney, Sue.
    Hinduism / Sue Penney.
        p. cm. -- (World beliefs and cultures)
    Includes bibliographical references and index.
    ISBN 1-57572-356-5
    1. Hinduism--Juvenile literature. [1. Hinduism.] I. Title. II. Series.

BL1203 .P46 2000
294.5--dc21

00-033479

Acknowledgments
The Publishers would like to thank the following for permission to reproduce photographs: Andes Press Agency/Carlos Reyes-Manzo, pp. 5, 10, 16, 22, 28, 29, 30, 35, 38, 39, 42; Ann & Bury Peerless, pp. 7, 12, 17, 20, 37, 43; Christine Osborne Pictures, pp. 6, 8, 9, 21, 23, 26, 36, 40, 41; Circa Photos Library, pp. 11; Circa Photos Library/John Smith, p. 11; Circa Photos Library/Bipin J. Mistry, p. 14; Circa Photos Library/William Holtby, p. 25; Circa Photos Library/Robyn Beeche, p. 25; FLPA/E. & D. Hosking, p. 4; Hutchison, pp. 24, 27, 31, 33; Mary Evans Picture Library, p. 13; Phil & Val Emmett, p. 34.

Cover photograph reproduced with permission of E. T. Archive.

Our thanks to Philip Emmett for his comments in the preparation of this book.

Some words are shown in bold, **like this.** You can find out what they mean by looking in the glossary.

Contents

Dates: In this book, dates are followed by the letters B.C.E. (Before Common Era) or C.E. (Common Era). This is instead of using B.C. (Before Christ) and A.D. (*Anno Domini*, meaning in the year of our Lord). The date numbers are the same in both systems.

Introducing Hinduism

▲ *Hinduism is often compared to the spreading roots of the banyan tree such as the one above.*

Hinduism is the oldest of the major religions in the world. No one really knows when Hinduism began, but it goes back at least 5,000 years. It developed gradually over a period of about 1,000 years in the area that today is northern India.

Hinduism has many different "branches" or sects. It is a way of life, not just a religion. Its followers have a wide range of beliefs and ways of worshiping. Different Hindus may believe quite different things without anyone saying that they are right or wrong.

Hindus often use the image of a banyan tree to describe their religion. A banyan tree is a kind of fig tree that grows in India. Hindus say that this is similar to their religion—it spreads in all directions and draws from many different roots, but its origins come from one main trunk.

Hinduism fact check

- Hinduism began in India more than 5,000 years ago.

- There have been many important leaders and teachers in Hinduism, but Hindus do not follow the teachings of any one person.

- Hindus worship in temples. They also have **shrines** at home.

- Hindus worship God, also called **Brahman,** through gods and goddesses. Images called **murtis** represent different aspects of the power of Brahman. They are treated with great respect, as if they were the god or goddess themselves.

- The oldest of the Hindu holy books are called the **Vedas.**

- About 800 million people in India are Hindu, and Hindus live in many other countries of the world. There are about one million Hindus in the United States, about 360,000 in the United Kingdom, and about 45,000 in Australia.

- The **symbol** used for Hinduism is made up of **Sanskrit** letters. Sanskrit is a very old language in which the Hindu holy books were first written. The letters spell the word **Aum.**

Sanatan dharma

Hindus do not usually use the word *Hinduism*. They describe what they believe as **Sanatan dharma,** which means "**eternal** truths." Hindus believe that their religion follows basic teachings that have always been true and always will be true. These truths are written down in the Hindu holy books. Hindus believe that the whole universe and everything in it follows these eternal truths, and therefore everything is Hindu. Most Hindus are not particularly interested in converting other people to follow their beliefs.

What do Hindus believe?

Hinduism teaches that there is one universal spirit called Brahman. Most Hindus say that Brahman can be translated as God. Hindus believe that Brahman is everywhere and in everything. Nothing would exist as it is if Brahman was not in it. They often use the illustration of saltwater to explain this. The salt cannot be seen, but it is present in even the tiniest drop of the water, and without it the water would be quite different. In the same way, Brahman is present in everything in the universe and makes everything what it is.

▲ *Hindus worship at a temple.*

Most Hindus say that the universal spirit can be seen most easily through gods and goddesses. The three main gods are Shiva, Vishnu, and Brahma. One of the most important goddesses is Shiva's wife. She has many names including Durga, Kali, Parvati, and Uma. As Durga and Kali, she is fierce and frightening. As Parvati and Uma, she is the goddess of motherhood. Many gods and goddesses appear in different forms to describe different parts of their personalities. This can be confusing, even for Hindus. However, most agree that all the gods and goddesses are different ways of describing Brahman.

Reincarnation

Belief in rebirth or **reincarnation** affects every part of a Hindu's life. Reincarnation is the belief that when a person dies, his or her soul moves on to another body. This may be another person or an animal or plant, as Hindus believe that the soul in everything is the same. Where your soul goes depends on how you live in this life. The aim of every Hindu is to break out of this cycle so that his or her soul can become part of Brahman. This is called **moksha,** which is a state of perfect happiness.

5

Hindu Gods and Goddesses

No one knows how many gods and goddesses there are in Hinduism. Some say there are thousands; some people say millions. Most Hindus believe the gods and goddesses are **symbols** or ways of describing **Brahman,** the universal spirit. Hindus believe Brahman cannot be described and can never be understood. They believe they are more likely to worship Brahman properly if they worship through a god or goddess they can understand. There are many stories about the gods and goddesses. Hindus believe these stories help people learn about themselves and life in general. They describe the gods' families and their good and bad tempers and feelings, just as if they were ordinary people.

Gods

Hindus believe that the three most important gods are Brahma the creator of the universe, Vishnu its preserver, and Shiva its destroyer. These three work together to maintain the cycle of life in the universe. Everything is made, lasts for a time, and is then destroyed so new things can be made. Brahma is not worshiped very much today, but Vishnu and Shiva are both popular gods. Ganesha, Shiva's son, is also worshiped regularly today.

Vishnu

Vishnu is worshiped under several names, because Hindus believe he has come to Earth in several different forms, called **avatars.** The stories say that if the world is in great danger, Vishnu comes to protect it. This has happened nine times. The two most important avatars were the gods Rama and Krishna.

▼ *Lakshmi, goddess of beauty and wealth, with Ganesha. He has the head of an elephant and is the god of wisdom and good fortune.*

Shiva

About a quarter of all Hindus worship Shiva. He can be frightening because he is the destroyer, but he is also thought of as kind and easy to please. In statues, Shiva is often dancing the dance of the universe—the movement that keeps the whole universe in motion.

Ganesha

In the god family, Ganesha is the son of Shiva and the goddess Parvati. In a fit of rage, Shiva cut off his son's head by mistake. Ganesha's head was replaced with an elephant's head. Ganesha is often worshiped today, because he is the god of wisdom and good fortune. Hindus setting out on a journey or starting something new often pray to Ganesha, and his image is often buried in the foundations of a new building.

A legend about Vishnu

Manu, the father of the world, was bathing in the river one day when a tiny fish begged to be rescued because bigger fish wanted to eat him. Manu took the fish home and dug a pond for him to live in. The fish grew and grew and eventually asked Manu to put him in the ocean. As Manu let him go, the fish warned him that there was going to be a great flood and Manu should build a boat to save himself. Manu did so, and the flood came. During the storm, the fish appeared again as a huge creature with golden scales and a horn. He caught hold of the ship's anchor rope and pulled it along for many years, until they came to rest on top of Mount Hemavat, which was still above the water. Manu anchored the ship there to wait for the end of the flood. Before he left, the fish told Manu that he was really Vishnu, and Manu had been saved so that the world would not be entirely destroyed.

Goddesses

The goddess of destruction is Shiva's wife. She has two names. As Durga, she is supposed to destroy demons. As Kali, she is frightening but is thought to bring peace of mind to the people who worship her, because she helps them overcome their fears. She is usually shown wearing a necklace of skulls around her neck and holding weapons in her six or eight hands.

Shiva's wife also has a gentle side. As Parvati or Uma, she is the beloved goddess of motherhood.

Lakshmi

Lakshmi is Vishnu's wife. She is the goddess of beauty and good fortune. She is often pictured standing on a lotus flower. Many Hindus pray to her at the festival of Diwali, which begins the financial year. They hope she will help them to prosper in the year ahead. Lakshmi is thought of as a wanderer who never stays long with anyone.

▼ *A **murti** of the mother goddess Kali, who helps people overcome their fears.*

A Brief History of Hinduism

Hinduism was not founded by one person or group of people. The religion developed gradually over a long period of time. It started so long ago that no one really knows how it happened. The history of Hinduism and the history of India are closely connected. Today, about 79 percent of the population of India—almost 800 million people—are Hindus.

▲ *The Great Bath at Mohenjo-Daro, part of the Indus Valley civilization that flourished around 2500 B.C.E., in what is now Pakistan.*

The very beginning

You can find the places mentioned in this book on the map on page 44.

The beginnings of Hinduism can be traced back to an ancient civilization that flourished in the Indus Valley between about 3000 and 1700 B.C.E. In the twentieth century, archaeologists discovered some of the remains of this civilization and proved that the people had a very organized lifestyle. They also found statues that show that the people worshiped a mother goddess and a bull. The remains of a huge bathing area show that bathing was an important part of their worship.

In around 1500 B.C.E., the region was invaded by people called **Aryans,** who worshiped nature gods—gods of the sun, moon, and stars. It seems that over many years the two forms of worship came together. People probably carried on worshiping their own gods, but they began to worship other gods, too. From about 1400 B.C.E., the Aryans composed special **hymns** to the gods. These were called **Vedas.** So this period of the Hindu religion is called the Vedic period.

The early days of Hinduism

The people of India probably carried on worshiping in very similar ways for about 1,000 years. Then, gradually, some people became dissatisfied. They began to look at the teachings of other religions. In the fourth and third centuries B.C.E., the teachings of Buddha Gautama became popular. The **Buddhist** Emperor Ashoka, who ruled most of India, encouraged the people of India to follow the teachings of Buddha. By the end of his reign in 232 B.C.E., almost all of India was Buddhist.

Hindu leaders realized that this was a serious challenge for Hinduism. It had to become more organized, and ideas began to change. People began to worship Shiva and Vishnu, rather than the nature gods they had been worshiping before. Worship of the gods in temples became less important as people began to worship more at home. This meant that people were more likely to worship one god who was particularly important to them, rather than many gods equally.

The Puranic period

The Puranic period lasted from about the fourth to the thirteenth century C.E. The name comes from the **Puranas,** important stories that were written down during that period. This was also the time when Hindu teachers began to put together some of the ideas and teachings of Hinduism that are still important today.

Between the twelfth and sixteenth centuries C.E., India was invaded three times by different groups of Mughals, who were **Muslims.** During this time, Hinduism became less popular again because, as Muslims, the Mughals did not agree with Hindu ways of worship, and many Hindu temples were destroyed.

 *Members of Hare Krishna participate in a festival procession.*

The past 200 years

During the past 200 years, the world has changed very rapidly. Hindu leaders have worked to make sure that Hindu beliefs stay constant. In the nineteenth century, a teacher named Vivekananda worked to present Hinduism as a world religion for the first time. In the 20th and early 21st centuries, Hinduism has developed in many countries, as Hindus have traveled to different parts of the world.

Hare Krishna

There are many different groups in Hinduism. They usually follow the teachings of a particular holy man, often called a **guru** or swami. One of the most well-known groups of Hindus in Western countries is the International Society for Krishna Consciousness (ISKCON), commonly called Hare Krishna. It came from India in 1954. Its leader was Bhaktivedanta Swami. His teachings are based on those of a Hindu holy man who lived in the sixteenth century C.E. These say that people are not really "alive," but are "sleeping" and do not understand the real meaning of life. They need to "wake up" to their real selves. They can do this by repeating a **mantra** or prayer, Hare Krishna. *Hare* means "God who forgives wrongdoings." People who belong to ISKCON are strict vegetarians. They live simple lives, believing that everything they do is an offering to the god Krishna.

The Caste System

The origins of the caste system

The **caste** system is the way that Indian society has worked for hundreds, probably thousand, of years. It divides people into groups. There is a story in the **Rig-veda** about how the caste system began. It says that the first man was named Purusha. He was sacrificed by the gods, and…

> *into how many parts was he divided? What did his mouth, arms, thighs and feet represent? The **Brahman** was his mouth, the **Kshatriya** his arms, the **Vaisyas** his thighs and the **Sudras** were born from his feet.*
> (*Rig-veda* 10.90.12)

Religion divided society into four groups or **varnas.** The first and most important varna, called Brahmans, were priests. The second varna, Kshatriyas, were soldiers. The people who ruled the country came from this group. The Vaisyas were shopkeepers, traders, and farmers. The last of the four groups were the Sudras, who were servants for the other three varnas. Over many years, these varnas divided into many smaller groups called **jatis.** A person's jati was determined by what job his or her family did. Jobs were passed on in families, so a son would do the same job as his father. Girls in those days did not work outside the home. Today, it is no longer the case that sons or daughters must do the same job as their parents, because people have more educational opportunities and usually more freedom of choice. However, they still stay in the same jati. People in some jatis are thought to be closer to God than those in others.

▼ *A Hindu priest distributes **prashad** at the end of worship.*

Harijans

Outside the four varnas were the **harijans.** They did the dirtiest jobs. For example, many Harijans worked with leather, which other Hindus would not do. For many years, other Hindus would not have anything to do with harijans. In the early years of the twentieth century, the Hindu leader Mahatma Gandhi worked hard to improve the lives of these people. He gave them the name harijans, which means "children of God."

The caste system today

The people in India have lived under the caste system for hundreds of years. In the past 50 years, things have changed. More people travel away from their home areas to live and work in cities. In factories and shops, people have to meet and talk with people who are not from their own varna. They cannot keep

▲ In many Indian villages, people live in very traditional ways.

the rules so strictly. Now many Brahmans are not priests, not all members of the army are Kshatriyas, and many people who are not Vaisyas own shops. Apart from Brahmans and Harijans, many people are not sure which varna they belong to, although they know what jati they are and what this means in their dealings with other people.

The law has changed, too. Partly because of the work done by Mahatma Gandhi, laws were passed to try to make Indian society more equal. However, it takes a long time to change the way people think, and changing the law is not always enough. In many villages in India, the caste system is still very strict. This means that people will not marry someone from a "lower" jati and anything they eat must have been prepared by someone from their own or a "higher" jati.

Niranjan's view

Niranjan, 13, lives in London.

There are lots of Hindus near where we live, and a lot of families belong to the same jati. Back in India years ago all my family were farmers, but my grandfather came to Britain, and my father worked very hard to get lots of jobs. Now he is a doctor at a hospital in London. About 20 years ago, people from the jati joined together and bought a church hall that wasn't being used any more. I go there on Saturday mornings for classes so that I can learn to read and write Urdu, which is what we speak at home. The adults use the hall for lots of other things as well. There's a group for old people, and I go to the youth club on a Friday sometimes. It's good to meet other people who are brought up in the same way as me.

Three Hindu Leaders

You can find the places mentioned in this book on the map on page 44.

Shankara (788–820 C.E.)

Shankara was born into a family of **Brahmans** and became a holy man when he was very young. He gave up his home and family and spent the rest of his life traveling and teaching in India. He founded temples in many different parts of India, and his beliefs and teachings attracted many followers.

Shankara's teaching was about **Atman**—the relationship between the soul that Hindus believe is in everything and the universal spirit, Brahman. He taught that Atman and Brahman are the same. They only seem to be different because human beings cannot understand Brahman. Only Brahman is real. Everything in the world only seems to be real. Shankara often used an example to illustrate this:

> A man goes into a dark room and sees a rope on the floor. He thinks it is a snake. For that man, the rope really is a snake until he discovers it is not.

Shankara taught that the way human beings see the world is the way the man sees the snake. Shankara's ideas are the foundation of a large part of Hindu teaching.

▼ *A statue of Ramakrishna at his birthplace in Bengal, India.*

Ramakrishna (1834–66 C.E.)

Ramakrishna was a great leader of Hinduism in the nineteenth century. He played a major part in reviving Hinduism and making it more structured. He came from a poor family and, at the age of 21, became a priest at the temple of the goddess Kali, near Calcutta, India. He became so involved in the worship that he often used to go into deep trances, becoming unconscious to everything around him. His holiness and the way he cared for people made him very famous. Many of his followers believed that he was an **avatar** of the god Vishnu.

When he died, he left behind many followers who continued his work. One of them was Vivekananda, who worked to present Hinduism as a world religion for the first time.

Mahatma Gandhi (1865–1948 c.e.)

Mohandas Karamchand Gandhi was one of the most important Hindus of the 20th century. He was born in India but trained in England as a lawyer. He began work in South Africa. There, he became aware of racial **discrimination,** and he became well-known as a writer and fighter for freedom. As a Hindu, he believed that all life is sacred, and this gave him the basis for his way of fighting. He insisted that protesters did not need to use violence. Throughout his life he taught the idea of **ahimsa—** nonviolence and respect for life.

In 1915, Gandhi returned to India and became an important national leader. During the 1930s, he played a large part in the negotiations for independence as India left the British Empire. As part of the independence settlement, the new country of Pakistan was created to be a **Muslim** country. In what is thought to be one of the largest movements of people in history, six and a half million Muslims moved to Pakistan, and more than five million Hindus moved from Pakistan to India.

This caused bitterness and fighting, and thousands of people were killed in riots. Gandhi used all of his influence to calm the fighting. He even went on a hunger strike, risking his own life to persuade people to stop. In January 1948, Gandhi

▼ *Encouraging the use of the spinning wheel was part of Ghandi's peaceful way to gain Indian independence from Britain.*

was shot dead by Nathuram Godse, a member of an extreme group that disagreed with Ghandi's teachings. More than three million people took part in his funeral procession. He is remembered and respected as a man of peace by people all over the world. The title Mahatma means "great soul," and is a way of saying that he showed how love can overcome evil.

Grief for Gandhi

When Gandhi was killed, India's Prime Minister Jawaharlal Nehru made a radio broadcast. This is part of what he said:

"The light has gone out of our lives and there is darkness everywhere. Our beloved leader, Bapu, as we called him, the father of the nation, is no more. The light has gone out, I said, and yet I was wrong. For the light that shone in this country was no ordinary light. In a thousand years that light will still be seen … for it represented the living, the **eternal** *truths, reminding us of the right path, drawing us from error, taking this ancient country to freedom."*

Hindu Holy Books

Hinduism has developed over about 5,000 years. In that time, hundreds of different Hindu holy books have been written. Some praise the gods. Some outline and describe the correct ways of worship. Some put forward and discuss Hindu beliefs. Most of these books were written in **Sanskrit,** which is one of the oldest languages in the world. Today, Sanskrit is not spoken anywhere and is only used for religious purposes. Some of these holy books are not often read now, but others are still very important.

The Hindu holy books are divided into two main groups. Some are called **shruti,** which means "heard." Hindus believe that these words were heard by wise men in the early days of the religion. Others are called **smriti,** which means "remembered." These are words that were handed down by word of mouth for hundreds of years before they were written down. A father would teach his son the words, the son would teach his own son, and so on. People in those days were used to remembering things, because very few people could read or write.

The two main groups of shruti texts are the **Vedas** and the **Upanishads.**

▲ *A priest reads the Vedas at home in front of his* **shrine.**

The Vedas

The Vedas are the oldest of the Hindu holy books. Hindus believe that the Vedas came from God and contain basic truths that never change. *Veda* means "knowledge" or "wisdom." The words the Vedas contain go back to about 1200 B.C.E., but they were not collected together and written down until about 1400 C.E. The most important Veda is the first. It is called the **Rig-veda** and contains more than 1,000 **hymns,** made up of verses called **mantras.** The hymns are really poems praising the 33 gods who control the forces of nature—the gods of the **Aryan** people. The other Vedas contain instructions to the priests about how worship should be carried out and descriptions of religious ceremonies. This is part of a hymn to the earth goddess, Prithivi:

You send us the water-laden cloud, O shining goddess. With your strength you hold the trees firmly in the ground when the lightning flashes and thunder-rain showers from the sky.
(*Rig-veda* 5.84.3)

The Upanishads

The Upanishads are the last part of each Veda. They were written down between about 400 and 200 B.C.E. The name comes from words that mean "sit down near," and this is how the teachings began. Young men who wanted to learn from the older, wise teachers would sit down around them, listen to what they were saying, and learn from it. The Upanishads contain discussions about the most important things that Hindus believe—for example, what **Brahman** is like—and about the soul in all things, **Atman.** Other holy books are of the smriti group.

The Laws of Manu

The books of the Laws of Manu are some of the most important law books for Hindus. No one really knows when Manu lived, but his words were written down by 300 C.E. There are 2,685 verses in the Laws of Manu. They contain instructions about how Hindus should live their lives and show how important it is to follow the teachings of Hinduism in everyday life. They include the punishments for certain crimes and rules that priests should follow. The Laws of Manu are very detailed, for example:

No guest should be allowed to stay in a Brahman's house without receiving hospitality, food, water, and a bed.

The Puranas

The **Puranas** were written down over a period of about 1,000 years, after about 500 C.E. *Puranas* means "olden times." They are part of the group of holy books that help to explain the Vedas. They contain many well-known stories and deal mainly with the worship of Brahma, Vishnu, Shiva, and Shakti. Altogether there are over half a million verses in the Puranas.

Prayers from the Vedas

Hearing the words of the holy books is still very important to many Hindus, even though they are now written down in books. One of the prayers in the Rig-veda is to Savitiri, the sun god. Many Hindus repeat this prayer every morning as part of their worship. It is known as the Gayatri mantra, or prayer.

In Sanskrit, the prayer looks like this, and the translation is written below.

ॐ भूर्भुवः स्वः । ॐ तत्सवितुर्वरेण्युं भर्गो देदस्य धीमहि । धियो यो नः प्रचोदयात्

*We **meditate** on the loving light of the god Savitri. May his brilliance, like that of the sun, stimulate our thoughts.*

The *Mahabharata* and the *Ramayana*

▲ *Dances of the stories from the holy books are popular.*

Hindus believe that the **shruti** holy books contain teachings that were revealed to holy men, as well as their ideas and thoughts after they had spent years studying the religion. Ordinary people found them difficult to understand, so other traditions developed. These were based on the same sort of teaching as the holy books but were in the form of stories that were easier to understand. In time, the stories themselves became part of the **smriti** holy books. Among the most important part of the smriti are two long poems. One is called the *Mahabharata,* the other is called the *Ramayana.* They contain stories that Hindus of all ages love to listen to. They also teach lessons about the religion.

The *Mahabharata*

The *Mahabharata* is the longest poem in the world. It has 100,000 verses. It was written by many different people over several hundred years. The poem is complicated, because it not only has a main story but it has many other stories that are included to teach important lessons. The main story is about two royal families. They are cousins. They quarrel over who should be the rightful ruler of the country. One family tricks the other, and war begins. There is a great battle. Before the battle begins, one of the royal princes, Arjuna, talks to the person who is driving his chariot. This person turns out to be the god Krishna in disguise. This is the most famous part of the poem and includes the *Bhagavad-Gita,* probably the best-loved part of all the Hindu holy books.

Bhagavad-Gita means "song of the Lord." It deals with some of the most difficult teachings of the Hindu holy books but in a way that is easy to understand and that all Hindus can relate to wherever and whenever they live. For many Hindus, the *Bhagavad-Gita* is the most important part of the holy books. In the story, Arjuna tells Krishna that he does not want to fight because the battle is against his cousins, and he does not want to kill his relatives. Krishna teaches the prince about his duty and about the right ways for people to worship.

The *Ramayana*

The *Ramayana* is shorter than the *Mahabharata* but still contains 24,000 verses. It is thought to be the work of a man named Valmiki and was probably written down about 100 C.E. It is divided into seven books, in which the main character, Rama, is an **avatar** of the god Vishnu. The characters are all "ideal." In other words, they are either all good or all bad. Prince Rama is a good son, a loving husband, a wise king. His wife, Sita, is beautiful, modest, and obedient to her husband. The demon Ravana is totally bad.

Stories in the *Ramayana*

In the story of the *Ramayana*, Rama's father promises his youngest wife two wishes. She asks for her own son, Bharata, to be made king instead of Rama and for Rama to be sent away for fourteen years. The king is heartbroken but must keep his promise to his wife. Rama obeys his father and goes to live in a far-off country with his wife and his brother. One day, while Rama and his brother are out hunting, Rama's wife, Sita, is kidnapped by the wicked demon Ravana. He keeps her prisoner on an island. The monkey-god Hanuman helps Rama find Sita, and Hanuman's monkey army helps Rama attack the island. They win a fierce battle against Ravana, in which Ravana is killed. Rama and Sita are able to return home. Rama is crowned king, and everything ends happily. Good wins over evil.

▲ *An old painting showing a scene from the* **Ramayana** *(notice Rama and Sita, seated, and Hanuman kneeling).*

The *Mahabharata* and the *Ramayana* can be understood in many different ways. For children, they are exciting stories. For adults, they can be understood on a much deeper level, teaching important lessons about the gods and the way to worship. Hindu actors and dancers often use the stories in their performances, because they are familiar to almost everyone.

From the *Bhagavad-Gita*

This extract from the *Bhagavad-Gita* shows that it is not the offering to the **murtis** itself that is important in worship, it is the spirit in which it is given.

> *Whoever offers me a leaf,*
> *a flower, a fruit, or water with devotion,*
> *That offering I will accept*
> *From the pure in heart,*
> *because it was offered with love.*

(*Bhagavad-Gita* 9.26–7)

Worship in the Home

What Hindus believe about worship

Hindus believe that **Brahman** is in everything. This means that every part of life can be part of worship if you do things carefully and with thought. Even everyday tasks such as cooking or cleaning can be part of worship if they are done with the right attitude and in the right way. Hindus also worship in special ways in temples and at home. This worship may include **meditation,** or repeating the names of God. It may include reading or listening to readings from the holy books. The most common form of worship is called **puja.** This means making offerings to the **murtis** in the **shrine,** a holy place.

Shrines in the home

Hindus normally have a shrine in their homes, where they worship at least once a day. Shrines can be very different, depending on what the family can afford. In some houses, the shrine room may be separate and beautifully decorated. In other houses, the shrine is a simple cupboard or shelf. Like the gifts offered to the murtis in worship, it is not the size or appearance of the shrine that matters, it is the spirit in which it is used. The most usual place to find a shrine is in part of the kitchen or the mother's bedroom.

The most important thing in a shrine is the murti, the image of a god or goddess. Sometimes there are pictures of other gods or goddesses, too. The shrine always has perfume and flowers so that the murti and pictures are in beautiful surroundings. Some shrines have a little bottle containing water from the Ganges River in India, which Hindus believe is a sacred river.

◀ *This family worships at their shrine. Notice this shrine has a picture of Ganesha.*

What happens in worship?

The rules about making puja, or worship, are written down in the Hindu holy books. At home, puja is often performed by the wife or mother in the family. She prepares for it carefully, often bathing and wearing clean clothes. Hindus believe that the murti in the shrine represents Brahman, so they treat it very carefully. During puja it is washed and dried and may be touched with colored powders. Sometimes flowers are hung around it. Small gifts such as a flower petal or a grain of rice are offered. It is not the size of the gift that is important, it is the love with which the gift is offered that really matters.

Part of the puja is repeating **mantras.** A mantra is usually a verse from one of the holy books. Mantras begin with the sacred Hindu word *Aum.* Sometimes *Aum* is used on its own as a mantra, too. The mantras are repeated over and over again. Hindus believe that this is a way to help them concentrate on God.

Puja usually takes place in the morning and evening. In many Western countries, where the adults in the family may have to leave early every morning for work, evening worship is more usual. While they are making puja, Hindus do not wear shoes. They sit cross-legged on the floor or stand up. They often put their hands together and lift them to their face or in front of their chest. Sometimes they kneel and touch the ground with their forehead. These are all ways of showing respect.

▲ *This girl is worshiping Krishna at the shrine in her home. Notice that the murti is blue, a color that Hindus believe is a symbol of holiness.*

Radha's view

Radha, 13, lives with her family near New York. This is how she describes worship at their family shrine.

In our house, we worship God through Ganesha. Hindus always pray to him before going on a journey and before starting anything new. Every morning, we take a bath and then all sit cross-legged on the floor in front of the shrine—Mom, me, and my brothers, Rama and Anil. On weekends, Dad is there, too. Mom washes the murti of Ganesha by sprinkling milk mixed with water over it and dries it by stroking it with a cotton ball. She dips another cotton ball in sandalwood paste and perfume and pats the image. Then she puts a small garland of flowers around its neck. We say prayers and leave little gifts in front of the image. I like the feeling that starting the day with worship gives me. When I get to school, I feel more confident about tackling new things because I know that Ganesha helps people to succeed.

19

Hindu Temples

There are thousands of temples in India. Some are similar to small villages, with many different buildings. Others are tiny **shrines** by the side of the road. Hindus believe that the variety of shrines is a way of showing that **Brahman** is everywhere and can be seen in many different ways. In Western countries, Hindu temples often are buildings that were originally used for other purposes. More new temples are being built as Hindu communities become more settled in local areas. Sometimes a temple is called a **mandir,** which is a **Gujarati** word.

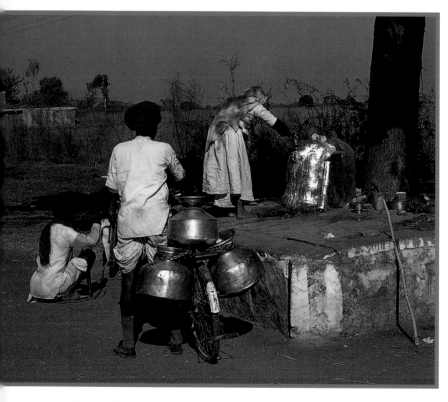

▲ In India, worshiping at a roadside shrine is part of everyday life.

Where are temples built?

Many important temples are built where stories say something happened in the life of a god. As a result, the place became a center of **pilgrimage,** so a temple was needed. Small roadside shrines often were built to remember an event or to ask a god's protection for travelers. A water supply is important, partly because people need water to wash themselves before they can worship. Also, many Hindu gods are associated with water, and water plays an important part in the religion.

Symbols in a temple

Temples include many objects that are **symbols.** Many temples fly a flag outside, which is a symbol of the presence of Brahman. Temples often have a tower. This is a symbol of the pillar that people in India once thought was at the center of the universe. A person going to the temple to worship goes from the outside to the shrine room, often in the center of the building. This is a symbol of the spiritual journey that a person makes in his or her life—the journey that Hindus believe leads to **moksha,** freedom from the cycle of birth and death. When Hindus go to worship in a temple, they take off their shoes before they go inside. This shows respect for the **murtis.** They also may ring a bell as a symbol of "waking up" the god.

Carvings

Many temples are beautifully carved inside and out. The carvings often show scenes from the life of the god. The temple doorway is often guarded by frightening carved creatures. Most of the gods have animals that are used for transportation. Sometimes the appropriate animal is included in the carvings near the doorway so that it is ready to take the god or goddess wherever he or she wants to go.

Inside a temple

What the rooms inside a temple look like depend on when and where it was built. A tiny shrine by the side of the road only has space for the murti and a few symbolic objects. Huge temples that have a large staff of people have rooms where they can live as well as many different shrine rooms, so that different murtis can be worshiped.

At the entrance to a temple there is always a place where worshipers can leave their shoes. Everyone going to worship removes his or her shoes both as a mark of respect and to keep the holy place clean. The main room is the shrine room, which is always at the heart of the building. It is usually carpeted and beautifully decorated with paintings and statues.

Especially in Western countries, the temple is an important focus of life for Hindus. If the building is large enough, the temple has other rooms that help it to serve as a community center. Youth and senior groups may meet there. Some larger temples have a hall where marriages can be performed.

The Aum symbol

The most important sound for Hindus is the word **Aum,** also spelled *Om*. It is pronounced as if it was written ah-oo-m. For Hindus, this is a holy sound because it represents the sound of God (ॐ). They also believe that it is the origin of all sound. Aum begins and ends all prayers, **mantras,** and the **bhajans** that are used in worship in a temple. The Mandukya **Upanishad** begins with the words "Everything is Aum. The past, the present, and the future, and that that is outside time. Everything is Aum." The symbol is often used in temple carvings and in articles used in worship.

▶ *The symbol for* Aum *at the feet of a murti can become part of worship.*

Worship in a Temple

▲ *Arti is a special part of worship in a temple.*

Hindus believe that the entire universe is a place of worship. Temples are seen as a special place where a god can be visited—a kind of house where a god or gods live. They regard going to the temple to worship in much the same way as people think of going to visit a friend at his or her home.

Some smaller temples have only one **murti.** In large temples, the main **shrine** has the murti of the god to whom the temple is dedicated. Other shrines are homes for the other murtis.

The murtis need priests to look after them, so a temple always has at least one priest. A priest who leads the worship is called a **pujari.** A priest who also offers advice to the people has the title **pandit.** Most temples have at least one room where the priest lives. A river or other supply of water is needed so people can perform the ritual washing before they worship.

How do Hindus worship?

Worship in a temple often begins before dawn. The worship centers around the murti, which is treated as a very respected guest or royalty. The murti is "woken up" by the priest, and prayers are said, beginning with the sacred word *Aum.* The murti is washed in milk or water and dried. It may have sandalwood or turmeric—a spice plant—paste put on it. It is dressed in red and gold clothes and has garlands of flowers placed around its neck. In some larger temples, the murti is put away at night in a separate "bedroom," so it needs to be moved back to the main shrine room in the morning. Hindus believe that even the least important murti should be worshiped at least once a day. More important murtis are worshiped several times a day.

After all the preparations are complete, the priest who leads the worship draws back the curtains. Hindus believe that this not only means that they can see the murti, but that they can be "seen" by God. This is a very special moment that Hindus call **darshan.**

The arti ceremony

During the arti ceremony, the priest lights five lamps in a steel tray. For each murti, he moves the tray in a clockwise circle from the bottom to the top of the murti. Then it is circled again from left to right. As he is doing this, the worshipers sing a special song and chant a prayer.

The priest then circles the arti tray in the direction of the three other walls of the temple, a way of worshiping the gods who are the guardians of the four main points of the compass. He sprinkles water over the worshipers, often from a special shell. This is a **symbol** to show that the blessings of **Brahman** are being given to them. The arti tray is carried around among the worshipers. Sometimes they put small gifts of money on the tray. They hold their hands over the flames and then move the palms of their hands over their eyes, forehead, and head. They believe that by doing this they receive power from the god. During the worship, **prashad** is distributed to the people. This is food that has been blessed by the god. Usually it consists of nuts, fruit, and sweets.

Worshipers may place a dot or stripes of special powder or paste on their foreheads. This is usually made of sandalwood or turmeric paste and is called **tilak.** It is a symbol of the soul that is within everyone. The shape of the tilak shows which god the person has worshiped. A similar mark is made by the pujari on the forehead of the murti. Tilak is not the same as the red dot that many Indian women wear on their foreheads, which shows they are married.

▶ *A young Nepalese girl receives tilak, a symbol or mark that shows she has been to worship.*

Why does the arti ceremony always have five lights?

The five flames on the arti tray are symbols. They represent the five elements of nature, which are necessary for human beings to survive. They are water, fire, earth, air, and space. The number five also symbolizes the five senses—sight, smell, taste, hearing, and touch. It is a way of saying that people should love and worship Brahman with their whole being.

Two Important Temples

▲ *Worshippers at the Pashupatinath temple, Nepal. Notice the cremation ghats at the side of the river.*

The Pashupatinath temple, Nepal

For Hindus who worship Shiva, Pashupatinath is one of the most important centers of **pilgrimage** in Asia. Thousands of Hindus go there for the Mahashivaratri celebrations in the month of Phalguna. Because it is so important, the Pashupatinath temple, unlike most Hindu temples, is closed to non-Hindus.

The temple stands on the banks of the Bagmati River, a sacred river, about three miles (five kilometers) outside Kathmandu, the capital of Nepal. The buildings there date from the seventeenth century C.E., and the site itself was used for worship for hundreds of years before that. Alongside the river are many **ghats** or platforms people use to bathe and for **cremations.** The ghats closest to the front of the temple are only used for royal cremations.

The central temple has three roofs that are covered in gold. Around them are several other buildings used by worshipers and the priests who live in the temple. There are many other smaller temples in the grounds of the main building. The grounds are dotted with stone columns, called **linga,** which are **symbols** of Shiva.

How Shiva saved the world—a Hindu story

The gods and demons wanted to be able to live forever. Vishnu told them that they must obtain a liquid called the nectar of immortality from the celestial ocean of milk. To do this they had to churn up the milk so that it would give up its treasures. They began to churn, using the great serpent Vasuki as a churning rod. They churned and churned for 100 years. The first gift that the ocean gave them was the goddess Lakshmi, carried out of the milk on a bed of lotus flowers. Other gifts followed. Then, as they churned, the great serpent began to spew out a deadly venom. He had 1,000 mouths, and all of them began pouring a poison that would kill everything that lived. Shiva leaped forward and swallowed the poison. He was so powerful that it could not harm him, but swallowing it stained his throat dark blue. By this act, he saved the entire world from extinction.

Stories and legends like this help Hindus understand the important teachings of their religion, and so help them worship at home and in temples all over the world. This story also explains why **murtis** that show Shiva as a person (rather than the linga that is his usual symbol show him with a blue throat.

The Shri Swaminarayan Temple, London

This modern temple was completed in 1995. It was inspired by the man his followers call His Divine Holiness Pramukh Swami Maharaja. He is the leader of a group of Hindus who follow the teachings of Lord Swaminarayan. The temple is the largest outside India and is the first traditional stone temple to be built in Europe.

You can find the places mentioned in this book on the map on page 44.

The stone for the temple—more than 3,085 tons (2,800 metric tons) — came from Bulgaria, and 2,204 tons (2,000 metric tons) of marble came from Italy. It was all shipped to India to be carved in the traditional ways before being brought to London and put together like a jigsaw puzzle. In planning the temple, the architects took into account Hindu teachings on respect for life. Materials were chosen because they were environmentally friendly, and the heating and lighting systems are energy-efficient. For example, because 226 trees were cut down and used in the building, 2,300 saplings were planted in the United Kingdom and India.

The temple has five beautifully carved **shrines** for the murtis. The prayer hall, the largest in the world to be built in the past 100 years, is where the **arti** ceremonies and prayer meetings take place five times each day. However, the temple is not just a center for worship. There is a visitors' center with an exhibition about Hinduism. The buildings also include rooms that can be used for meetings, educational activities, and a marriage hall. There is also a sports hall, which was included with the idea that "if the young come to play they will in time come to pray."

▼ *The Swaminarayan Temple is the largest Hindu temple outside India.*

Pilgrimage

A **pilgrimage** is a journey that someone makes because of his or her religion. Many Hindus believe that making a pilgrimage is part of their religious duty. They may want to ask for something special or give thanks for something good that has happened to them. They may want to visit a place where the god they worship appeared to people or where a miracle happened. Most Hindus believe that by going on a pilgrimage to a special place they will achieve a better **karma.** Karma is the belief that actions from previous lives affect this life and future lives. Good actions in this life will help a person to be reborn to a better life next time.

You can find the places mentioned in this book on the map on page 44.

Places for pilgrimage

There are hundreds of places for pilgrimage all over India that may be visited by thousands of pilgrims at any one time. There are 24 main temples in India, of which twelve are more important than the others. Four of these twelve are the most important of all. They are thousands of miles (kilometers) apart at the four "corners" of India. Puri is on the east coast, Dwarka is on the west coast, and Badrinath is in the far north of India. These are **shrines** to Vishnu. Rameshwaram, on the south coast, is a shrine to Shiva.

Many Hindus spend most of their lives saving up to be able to visit all four of these temples. They may be poor and have great difficulties on the journey, but they believe that putting up with the hardships is part of serving **Brahman.** For this reason, some Hindus believe that a pilgrimage has more value if the pilgrim walks to the shrine. This may mean a walk of hundreds of miles (kilometers) over weeks or months, but they believe that the effort makes the pilgrimage more worthwhile. When they arrive at the temple or shrine, many pilgrims crawl around it on their hands and knees. This is a **symbol** that they are sorry for the things they have done wrong in their lives.

◀ *Worshipers at the temple at Puri on the east coast of India.*

Worship

When they arrive at the shrine, the worship is of a similar pattern to worship anywhere else. At the popular shrines, hundreds of people may wait for hours to gain **darshan**—the view of the **murti**. The offerings they give to the god they have come to worship are the same kinds of offerings they would give in worship at home—food, flowers, or money.

Holy rivers

Water is necessary for life. Hindus believe that rivers are a symbol of Brahman, who gives life. Bathing in a holy river is a symbol of inner cleansing—washing away **sin.** There are seven holy rivers in India, but the most famous is the Ganges River.

Varanasi

The most important place on the Ganges River is Varanasi, sometimes called Benares. This is where the god Shiva is believed to have lived. It is has been a center for Hindu teaching for thousands of years. On the banks of the river are special platforms called **ghats** that have steps that allow pilgrims to reach the river to bathe or offer **puja.** Every Hindu hopes to be in Varanasi when he or she dies, and some of the ghats are used for cremating dead bodies. After the body has been burned, the ashes are scattered in the Ganges River. The ashes of people who have died elsewhere are often scattered there, too. Hindus believe that this will help the person to achieve **moksha,** breaking out of the cycle of rebirth.

The Ganges River

The Ganges River flows from the Himalayas to the Bay of Bengal and is 1,560 mi (2,510 km) long. It is not the longest or the largest river in India, but Hindus believe that it is the most sacred river in the world. They treat it as the goddess Ganga come to Earth. The source of the river is called the Cow's Mouth. It flows out of an ice cave almost 10,300 ft (400 m) high and begins as a river almost 100 ft (30 m) across. Along the length of the river, and especially at Allahabad and Varanasi, millions of Hindus bathe in its waters. They believe that drinking even one drop of its water will rid them of all the sins they have committed in this life and in previous lives.

▲ *A holy man bathes at the source of the Ganges River in India.*

Celebrations—Diwali

For almost all Hindus, Diwali is the most important festival in the year. It takes place at the end of the month of Ashwin—September/October in the Western calendar—and carries on into the month of Kartik, which is October/November in the Western calendar. Not all Hindus celebrate Diwali in the same way. Even in India, because it is such an enormous country, customs can vary greatly. Celebrations in other countries can be even quite different. In some places, it is a three-day festival, but it usually lasts for five days. Diwali includes the beginning of the financial year.

Divas

Throughout the festival, Hindus decorate their homes, temples, and other buildings with rows of lights. In the past, small clay lamps called **divas** were used. Diwali is a short form of the word *Dipivali,* which means "rows of lights." Often, small electric lights are used instead of lamps. Glitter and tinsel are used for decorations as well.

◀ *Lighting candles is part of the Diwali celebration.*

Yamu's view

Yamu, 12, lives with her parents, grandparents, cousins, and their parents in Bombay, India.

On the first day of Diwali, we light a single clay lamp. This flame is for Yama, the spirit of death. Sometimes we have a few firecrackers or sparklers that night, but the main festival begins the next day. We all get up early and wash and put on new clothes before we make **puja** at home. This second day is called Naraka-chaturdashi, and we remember Vishnu's victory over the evil Naraka-Asura. On the third day, we make special offerings to Lakshmi. My cousin Sita and I draw patterns called rangolis in colored powder on the floor, and in the evening we make special puja. All the doors are open so that Lakshmi can come in, and after puja we set off fireworks to frighten away evil spirits. On the fourth day, married women get presents from their husbands. Last year, my father bought my mother a beautiful red **sari** with a matching blouse piece. I think the best day is the fifth, which we call sister's day. Sita and I make a fuss of our brothers and help cook special foods for them, then in the evening, they give us presents.

Stories of Diwali

Diwali is a special time for remembering Lakshmi, the goddess who brings good fortune. She is supposed to visit houses that are clean and tidy, and some people believe that the divas and other decorations light the way and welcome her to the house. Lakshmi is the goddess of wealth. Hindus hope that by welcoming her they will have a prosperous new year, as she leaves her wealth wherever she goes. Diwali comes at the end of the financial year, so people who own shops and businesses make sure that their account books are up to date and that all their debts are paid. Diwali is a time for closing personal "accounts," too—for example, making up any quarrels or arguments they may have had. This means that everyone can make a fresh start for the new year and hope that, with Lakshmi's help, it will be a good one.

Another story told at Diwali is from the *Ramayana*. It is about how Prince Rama won the battle against the evil Ravana and his army and found and rescued his wife, Sita. They returned home and Rama was crowned king. The people of the country were delighted to see the popular prince return, and lamps were lit to line the streets for Rama's victory procession.

There are also stories about how the god Vishnu won a battle with a wicked giant called Naraka Asura. In another story, Vishnu outwitted a very powerful king named Bali. In different parts of India, people think that some of these stories are more important than others. The stories are remembered in the celebration, so this explains why the festival is celebrated differently in different areas.

Diwali is a family festival. People give each other presents and share meals with friends and relatives. Sending cards for Diwali is becoming more popular, especially with Hindus who live in Western countries. There are firework displays and bonfires, with singing and dancing. The idea is to show that darkness can be driven away by light. This is a **symbol** that shows that evil can be driven away by good.

▲ *Lakshmi is the goddess who brings good fortune.*

Celebrations—Navaratri and Dassehra

Navaratri

Navaratri takes place in the month of Ashwin—September/October in the Western calendar, just after the **monsoon** rains. Its name means "nine-nights," the length of the festival. Celebrations take place among Hindus all over the world. Navaratri has different names in different places. In Gujarat, western India, it is called Navaratri. In eastern India, it is called Durga-**puja.** In northern India, the whole festival lasts an extra day and is called Dassehra. As with other Hindu festivals, different groups of Hindus recall different stories in their celebrations. Most of the celebrations honor the Goddess of Motherhod. She has several different names. In this festival, she is worshiped as Durga, a fierce soldier riding into battle on a lion.

Anyone who worships Durga as their special goddess celebrates the festival with great care. Although fierce, Durga also is thought to care for people, so she is the **symbol** of mothers. In the *Ramayana,* Prince Rama prays to Durga when his wife, Sita, is captured. Navaratri is an important time for families. In particular, girls who have been married during the past year try to return home and are given presents.

▲ *Dancing at the festival of Navaratri.*

In northern India, there are open-air plays during Navaratri that dramatize parts of the *Ramayana* story. In other places, people dance round a **shrine** of Durga, sometimes built especially for the festival. The shrine is a box with a cone-shaped top, and has pictures of the different appearances of the goddess on each side. The two traditional dances are a circle dance called "garba" and a dance with sticks, called "dandya ras." People dance and sing **hymns** to the goddess. The festivities can go on well into the night. Some people manage to do this every night for nine nights! Hindus believe that the festival is a time when they are given energy from the goddess, which they can use to overcome the evil they meet in their own lives. At the end of each night of the festival, there is an **arti** ceremony, and **prashad** is shared.

Dassehra

Dassehra means "tenth day." It falls on the day after the end of Navaratri. It is also known as Vijaya Dasami, which means "the tenth day of victory." During Navaratri, Hindus worship God through a **murti** of Durga. At Dassehra, this murti is taken to the nearest river and washed. Hindus believe that as it disappears under the water, it takes all their unhappiness and bad luck with it, and the river washes it all away. This makes Dassehra a very happy festival.

At Dassehra, Hindus also remember the story of the battle between Prince Rama and the wicked Ravana. Rama won the battle with the help of his brother, Lakshmana, and Hanuman the monkey-god, after he prayed to Durga for help. In many places, statues of Ravana are burned. In New Delhi, the capital of India, there is an enormous fireworks display at Dassehra. Wooden statues almost 100 ft (30 m) high of Ravana and his two brothers are packed with fireworks and burned.

▲ *Celebrants take the murti of Durga to the river to be washed.*

In all Hindu festivals, there is a serious lesson behind all the enjoyment. The *Ramayana* is the story of how good wins over the powers of evil and reminds people of **Brahman's** love. During Dassehra, Hindus try to settle any quarrels they may have had during the past year.

Durga and Mahishi

This is a story about Durga that Hindus remember at Navaratri.

Once there was a buffalo demon named Mahishi. He thought he could do anything he liked, because Brahma, the creator god, had promised him that he only could be killed by a woman. Mahishi was so conceited that he did not think any woman would ever be strong enough to kill him. The other gods begged Shiva to help. The goddess Durga agreed to the battle, and was armed with special weapons by the gods. Mahishi laughed when he saw her, but as she killed some of his demons, he knew he was really in danger. He changed into his buffalo form and charged her, but she was not hurt. Then, as he turned back into his demon form, Durga stabbed him with a spear. Mahishi was dead! Good had triumphed over evil, again!

Celebrations—Holi and Raksha Bandhan

▲ *A procession celebrating Holi. Notice the colored powder everywhere.*

Holi

Holi is a spring festival. It is celebrated by Hindus all over the world, although they remember different stories in their celebrations. It takes place in the spring—February or March in the Western calendar, Phalguna in the main Indian calendar.

The stories that Hindus tell most often at Holi are about Krishna. When he was young, he often used to play tricks on people. So Holi is a time for practical jokes. In Hindu countries, everyone joins in the fun—a favorite trick with children is to throw colored powders and water over people in the streets. There are often water fights as people join in. In countries where most people are not Hindu, children cannot usually "attack" people in the streets, but water fights among children are common. The custom remembers Krishna's friendship with some milkmaids, called gopis, and the story of how his favorite gopi, Radha, once threw colored dye over him when they had gone out for a walk. The story has a religious meaning, because it shows how well Krishna and Radha got along, so it reminds people that they must have a close and loving relationship with **Brahman.**

Where the name comes from

A more serious story gives the festival its name. Once there was a king who was very full of his own importance. He demanded that all his people worship him like a god. His own son, who was named Prahlada, was a devoted worshiper of Vishnu. He knew that his father was not a god, and it would be wrong to worship him. The wicked king was very angry when Prahlada refused to worship him, and he ordered that Prahlada be thrown into a pit full of poisonous snakes. Everyone expected him to die, but Vishnu protected him and he was unharmed. Next, his father arranged for Prahlada to be trampled on by a herd of elephants while he was asleep. Again, Vishnu protected him and he was not harmed.

Then the king asked for the help of his equally wicked sister, Holika. She had magical powers, which meant she would not be harmed by fire. She took Prahlada with her onto the top of a huge bonfire, expecting him to be burned to a crisp. Instead, Prahlada chanted the names of Brahman over and over again, and Vishnu protected him. Holika did not know that her magic powers only worked when she was in the fire alone, so they vanished, and she disappeared into the flames. The lesson of the story is that Prahlada, who trusted Brahman, was saved. Holika, who thought she had powers of her own, was destroyed. Holika gives the festival its name.

To remember this story, many Hindus celebrate Holi with a huge bonfire. Mothers sometimes carry their babies around this bonfire in a clockwise direction, as a **symbol** that they hope Agni, the god of fire, will bless the baby with a long and happy life. It is a custom to heat coconuts next to the fire and then eat them.

Raksha Bandhan

Raksha Bandhan is a popular festival that takes place on the day of the full moon in Shravan—July or August in the Western calendar. It celebrates the relationship between brothers and sisters. *Raksha* means "protection," *Bandhan* means "tie." At Raksha Bandhan, a girl ties a colored silk or cotton bracelet called a rakhi around her brother's wrist. As she does so, she says a short prayer that he will be blessed in the year ahead. Then she gives him a sweet. In return, the brother gives her a gift and promises to look after her and protect her. If a girl does not have a brother, it is usual for a cousin to be given the rakhi, instead.

▲ *At the festival of Raksha Bandhan, a girl ties a bracelet around her brother's wrist.*

Indra and Bali

The custom of giving a rakhi comes from a story about the god Indra. He had been fighting with a wicked demon king named Bali and had lost the battle. Bali had driven Indra out of his kingdom. Indra's wife was very upset about this, so she went to ask the god Vishnu if he would help. Vishnu gave her a bracelet made of cotton threads to tie around Indra's wrist. The bracelet had special powers, and when Indra next fought with Bali, it protected him. He won the battle and was able to drive Bali out and win back his kingdom.

Celebrations—Other Festivals

Hindus celebrate many festivals throughout the year. Some people say that every day there is a Hindu festival somewhere! Most festivals involve making special **puja.** Some festivals are important in a particular area or to worshipers of a particular god.

▲ *The solemn festival of Mahashivaratri honors Shiva.*

Mahashivaratri

Mahashivaratri is a solemn festival that honors Shiva. It takes place on the night of the new moon in Phalguna—January/February in the Western calendar. Mahashivaratri means "great night of Shiva," and Hindus believe that on this night, Shiva performs his special dance. This is the dance that provides the energy that keeps the universe moving—it destroys, but this means that new things can be created. Dancing Shiva is called Shiva Nataraja—Shiva the Lord of the Dance.

During the festival, **murtis** of Shiva are given special attention. Shiva murtis often show him dancing and holding his trident—a three-pronged spear. Shiva also has three horizontal lines across his forehead, and his followers have these placed on their foreheads, too, as a sign that they worship him. A **symbol** of Shiva is the **linga,** a stone column. Hindus pour milk over this as part of the ceremony.

The Shiva linga

This is the story of how the linga became a symbol of the greatness of Shiva.
One day, when the world was young, the gods Brahma and Vishnu were having an argument about which of them was greater. Suddenly a column of light appeared in front of them. They decided to settle the argument by having a race to see who could reach the end of the column first. Brahma turned himself into a goose. He flew high up in the sky, but he could not find the end of the column. Vishnu turned himself into a boar, nosing deep into the earth to find the other end. He did not succeed either. Then a booming voice said, "I am the Lord Shiva! You will never find my beginning or my end, because I am so great!" Brahma and Vishnu forgot their argument and began to worship Shiva.

Ramnavami

Ramnavami is the birthday festival of the god Rama. It takes place in spring. Rama, the hero of the *Ramayana*, is a very popular god for Hindus. He is often worshiped at the **shrines** in people's homes, but if they can, Hindus go to the **mandir** for Ramnavami to worship there, too. There are readings from parts of the *Ramayana*. A special part of the worship is the singing of the Ramanama, which is a list of all the names of Rama. An image of the baby Rama is placed in a cradle in the mandir. It is kept covered until midday, when Rama is said to have been born. In some places in India, the celebrations include images of Rama and his wife, Sita, being carried in procession through the village.

Like many other Hindu festivals, Ramnavami is a day of **fasting.** Fasting often means eating and drinking nothing, but for Hindus it means going without certain foods, such as meat, fish, onions, garlic, rice, wheat, and pulses—the seeds of certain plants. Foods that are allowed on fast days include fresh fruit, milk, and **ghee.** These are foods that many poor Hindu families could not normally afford, so eating them is a way of making festivals more special.

Janmashtami

Janmashtami takes place in Shravan and usually falls in August in the Western calendar. It celebrates the birthday of the god Krishna. The stories say that he was born at midnight, so many Hindus spend all night in the temple. They sing **hymns** in praise of Krishna, and there is dancing. At midnight, everyone gathers in front of the cradle that holds an image of Krishna. They perform the **arti** ceremony, then share **prashad**—gifts of fruit and specially cooked sweets that they believe have been blessed by the god.

▼ Shown here are decorations for Janmashtami, the celebration of the birth of Krishna.

They drink a traditional drink called charnamrit, which is a sweet mixture of milk, yogurt, sugar, water, and honey.

In many temples, nonstop repeated readings of the *Bhagavad-Gita* are organized for the eight days and nights before the festival. It takes about three hours to read the *Bhagavad-Gita* all the way through. People take turns, with reserves in case anyone is ill. The readings are timed to finish at midnight on Krishna's birthday.

Family Occasions—Childhood

Samskars

Special ceremonies are performed throughout a Hindu's life. These are called **samskars.** Altogether, there are sixteen samskars that should be performed at various times. Like most important Hindu ceremonies, the correct way of performing them is described in the holy books. The first six samskars take place during childhood.

Before birth

The first samskar takes place when a couple are hoping for a baby, before it has been conceived. They pray about the kind of child they would like. The next two samskars are performed during pregnancy. They are prayers that ask **Brahman** to protect mother and baby, so the child will be born healthy.

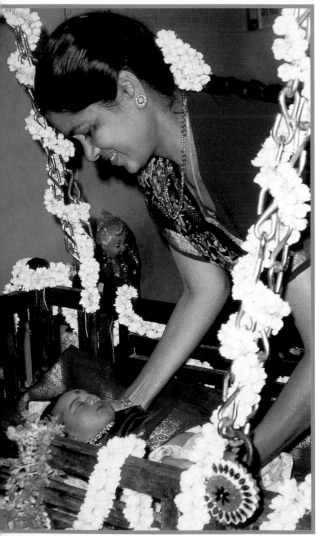

▼ *The baby is placed in a cradle before the naming ceremony.*

Birth

The fourth samskar takes place right after the birth. The baby is washed, and the father or a priest places a few drops of honey and **ghee** in the child's mouth, using a gold ring. He says, "May your life be as precious as gold. This will depend on your good thoughts, speech, deeds, and behavior." Hindus make a careful note of the exact time and place of birth, which will be used by the priest who prepares the baby's **horoscope.** A horoscope is a way of telling the future based on the positions of the stars. Many Hindus use horoscopes in their life to figure out the best times for events.

The naming ceremony

The baby is usually given a name when he or she is twelve days old. Hindus believe that the right name will bring the child luck. A priest often is asked to suggest a suitable initial or first syllable. The baby is dressed in new clothes and placed in a cradle. The ceremony itself is very simple—the name is announced by the eldest woman in the family, and the father says into his baby's ear, "Now your name is …" Everyone sings songs, and a special sweet made of fruit, nuts, and sugar is given to friends and relatives who have come to the ceremony.

The next three samskars are prayers and ceremonies that take place as the baby grows. The ninth samskar takes place when the baby is about a year old and has the first haircut. For a boy, this means having his whole head shaved, a **symbol** of removing any bad **karma** from his previous life.

The thread ceremony—upanayana

The tenth samskar is a very important ceremony for boys in the three higher **varnas.** Members of the lower **castes** do not take part in this ceremony. The boy's age may vary, but normally he is between seven and twelve. A sacred thread—a loop of cotton—is hung over his left shoulder. It hangs down to his right hip. This thread is a **symbol** that he is joining the religion. After he has received it, a boy is counted as a man. He can read the holy **Vedas** and carry out religious ceremonies. He wears the thread for the rest of his life, changing it at festivals. After the ceremony, there is a feast for family and friends, and the boy receives presents.

▲ *Adult Hindus prepare a boy for the sacred thread ceremony.*

A **guru** (religious teacher) prepares the boy for this ceremony and prays for the boy before giving him the thread. Then he becomes the boy's teacher while he studies the holy books. Some boys spend several years studying. The thread ceremony is thought of as a spiritual (religious) birth, so it is the reason why members of the three highest varnas are sometimes called "twice-born." They have had a spiritual birth as well as their birth as a baby.

The sixteen samskars

- The sixteen samskars can be described as markers of the stages of life. Because these are times when the person's life is changing, they are seen as dangerous times. Therefore, the person needs the protection of special prayers.
- The first three samskars take place before birth.
- The next six take place during a baby's first year.
- The tenth and eleventh occur when a boy begins his education and when he completes it.
- The next two occur when a couple get engaged and when they marry.
- The fourteenth and fifteenth occur when someone retires and when they reach the stage of giving up the world (see page 41).
- The final samskar is performed by other people. It occurs after a person has died and has been **cremated,** when his or her ashes are scattered into running water.

Family Occasions—Marriage

Hinduism teaches that marriage is important, so that there can be children to carry on the family. Hindu marriages are usually "arranged." This means that the parents and older relatives choose or suggest a suitable partner. Marriage is seen as a joining of two families, so it is important that the decision is not just left to individuals. The parents often take the advice of a priest and may use the couple's **horoscopes** to make sure that they are well matched. In the past, couples did not meet until their wedding day. Now things are not usually as strict as they once were, and the young person may suggest a possible partner or may have met the chosen partner a few times before the wedding.

The betrothal

The first step of a marriage is the ceremony to announce the engagement, or betrothal. The men from both families meet. There are readings from the **Vedas,** and prayers are said. The ceremony ends with a meal.

The wedding

The wedding ceremony usually lasts about an hour, but the celebration often goes on for several days. The wedding may take place in the bride's home, at a hall, or the temple may be used, depending on the number of guests. The bride wears special eye makeup, and a dye made of **henna** is used to make patterns on her hands and feet. She wears a new red and gold **sari** and a lot of gold jewelry. Preparing the bride for the ceremony takes several hours. The bridegroom also offers special **puja** to help him to prepare for his new life.

Both the bride and groom wear garlands of flowers.

First, the bride's father welcomes the bridegroom. The bridegroom sits under a special canopy, a decorated covering. He is given presents as **symbols** of happiness and a good life.

◄ *Hindus attend an outdoor wedding in India. Notice the money that the couple has received.*

Then the bride arrives, usually wearing a veil so her face cannot be seen. Sometimes a veil or light curtain is held between the bride and groom. This is removed during the ceremony. The couple sit in front of a special fire that is a symbol that **Brahman** is present at the marriage. Their right hands are tied together, and holy water is sprinkled on them when the bride's father "gives" her to the bridegroom. There are prayers and offerings of rice.

The couple make offerings of wood, **ghee,** and grain to Agni, the god of fire, before they walk carefully around the fire saying prayers. Then they take seven steps together near the fire. The seven steps stand for food, strength, wealth, happiness, children, the seasons, and lasting friendship. At each step, the couple stop and make promises to each other. While they do this, they are joined by a piece of cloth that is a symbol that they are being joined as husband and wife. Once they have taken the steps together, they are married. There are more prayers and readings, and flower petals are thrown, before the guests give their wedding presents. Then everyone shares a meal. After she is married, the bride is a member of her husband's family.

▲ A Western Hindu couple celebrates their wedding.

Divorce is permitted by Indian law, but strict Hindus do not accept any ending of a marriage except when one of the partners dies. Divorce is seen as a disgrace to both families.

Ashramas

According to Hindu teaching, life for males is divided into four stages called **ashramas.** When the teaching is observed strictly, the first ashrama is called the student, which begins with the sacred thread ceremony. It continues until the person is ready to set up a home and family, at which stage he should marry. This second stage is called the householder and lasts until about the age of 50. At this age, a man is expected to leave his family and friends and go and live in a peaceful place on his own. This stage is called the forest-dweller, and it is a preparation for the last stage, which is called the holy man. A holy man has no fixed home and as few possessions as possible. He has no responsibilities, so that he can concentrate entirely on his religion. Today, not everyone observes these stages strictly. Young people may not be able to afford to spend ten or fifteen years studying, and not all men want to spend the last years of their lives away from their families.

Family Occasions—Death and Reincarnation

Reincarnation

To understand Hindu teaching about death requires an understanding of **reincarnation,** an important part of Hindu belief. Reincarnation is the belief that when the body dies, the soul—Hindus call it **Atman**—moves on to another being. Hindus believe that the Atman in everything is the same—there is no difference between the Atman in a plant or animal or in a human being. Hindus believe that the Atman goes through a series of steps that begins in plants and animals and goes on to human beings. When a man or woman dies, his or her Atman is normally reborn in another person. This continual cycle of birth and death is called **samsara.**

▼ *This is a Hindu funeral procession in India.*

Karma

The movement of Atman after death depends on how a person lived. This is called the law of **karma.** *Karma* means "action." Good karma in a person's life means he or she may be reborn into a higher state in the next life. Bad karma in a person's life means he or she may be reborn into a lower state in the next life. There is no idea in Hinduism of being judged by **Brahman,** because how a person lives determines whether the next life is a step up or a step down. Steps may be missed, depending on the karma. Some Hindus believe that doing something very bad will cause the soul to be reborn in an animal. The soul then has to work its way up to a human being again. Doing something very good may mean the soul is given a "rest" before being reborn.

Moksha

The end of samsara is called **moksha.** This is what every Hindu hopes to achieve. The soul breaks out of the cycle of rebirth and joins with Brahman. Hindus say that this is similar to a river merging with the sea. It only can happen when the soul becomes completely pure, unaffected by anything that happens on Earth. Then the soul can go back to being part of Brahman, where it began.

Hindu funerals

These beliefs mean that Hindus see death as a welcome release, because it just means leaving behind a body that is no longer needed. When someone dies, his or her body is washed and wrapped in a cloth called a **shroud.** A garland of flowers may be placed on the shroud, then the body is put on a special stretcher. It is taken to be **cremated** on a **funeral pyre.** Where possible, the pyre is built on a **ghat** next to one of the sacred rivers. If there is no running water nearby, there is a cremation ground outside the town or village.

The eldest son or nearest male relative walks around the funeral pyre three times carrying a lighted torch. This sets a boundary around the pyre and is believed to encourage the soul to be released upwards into the atmosphere. Then he lights the fire. **Ghee** is used to help the flames burn. Families who can afford it include blocks of sweet-smelling sandalwood in the pyre. The people say prayers, and readings from the holy books remind the mourners that everyone who dies will be reborn. The closest male relative stays until the fire has gone out. Then he collects the ashes. All Hindus hope that they will be in Varanasi when they die and that their ashes will be scattered on the Ganges River. They believe that this will save them many future rebirths.

In many Indian cities, and in the West, bodies are not burned in the open air but are taken to a crematorium. Important customs such as walking around the body with a lighted torch are carried out at the funeral home. The ashes are collected after the body has been cremated. Many Hindus who live in other countries have the ashes of their relatives flown back to India so that they can be scattered on the Ganges River.

▶ *Ashes are scattered on the Ganges River.*

The kriya ceremony

The kriya ceremony takes place ten or twelve days after a funeral. Rice and milk are made into offerings. These are not just for the person who has died, but for everyone in the family who has died in the past. Rice is an important food, and milk comes from the sacred cow. Once this ceremony has been held, the person's soul is believed to have been rehoused in another body. The days of mourning, when the family did not go out, are over. The family can return to normal.

What It Means to Be a Hindu

As an individual

Hinduism is about the way a person lives, but beliefs are a very individual matter. One Hindu may have very different beliefs from another, without being right or wrong. This is partly due to the Hindu belief in **dharma,** usually translated as "duty." Hindus believe that every person has his or her own dharma. A person's dharma depends on who the person is, their background, the **jati** the person belongs to, and many other things. Dharma includes such things as worshiping **Brahman,** working to the best of a person's ability, not hurting other people and animals, and so on.

The four goals of life

The first goal in life for Hindus is to do their dharma to the best of their ability. The second goal is **artha**—being able to provide for your family. The third goal is **kama**—being able to enjoy good things in life in a moderate way. When these three goals have been achieved, the fourth goal should be **moksha,** the freedom from rebirth that every Hindu hopes to achieve. These four goals are a very important part of life for every Hindu.

It is part of each person's dharma to choose the way in which he or she worships in order to achieve moksha. The *Bhagavad-Gita* mentions four **yogas,** or paths, that people may use in their search for moksha. They are the path of knowledge, the path of **meditation,** the path of devotion, and the path of good works. Each path is open to anyone. Hindus do not have to choose only one. They can use any or all of them at different times in their lives. The most important thing is to reach moksha. How you get there is not important. The most popular path is the path of good works called **karma**-yoga.

◄ *A family makes **puja** at a temple in London.*

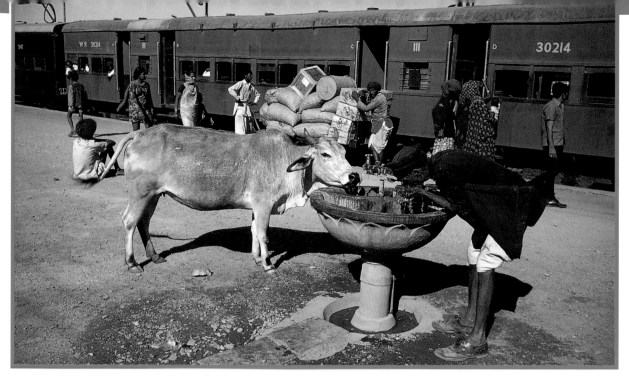

Respect for life

The teaching that **Atman** in all things is the same means that Hindus have a great respect for all living things. Because of this, many Hindus are vegetarians. In particular, no Hindu eats beef. This is because one of the things that links the whole community in India is respect for cows. Throughout all of India, cows are holy. Cows are milked, and their dung is used as fertilizer and dried for use as fuel. They are never harmed by people. They wander where they like, even in towns and cities, and there are severe penalties for killing or injuring a cow, even by accident. No one knows what this respect for the cow is based on. Some people think that it is because the white cow is a symbol of Atman.

▲ *In India, cows wander where they like.*

In the world

During the past 100 years, people have moved a lot around the world. So now there are Hindus in many countries. The teaching about dharma means Hindus place great value on education, and both men and women are found in professions such as teaching and medicine. Hindus who live in highly developed countries are very aware of the problems faced by people who live in the countries from which many of their families came. It is common for people to send money back, either to members of their families, or to improve facilities for the community.

The Brihadaranyaka Upanishad

The fact that Hindus care for the world and the people in it is only part of their belief. The most important Hindu teaching is that there is more to living than just life, and death is not the end. A famous quotation from the Hindu holy books sums up what it means to be a Hindu:

From the unreal
lead me to the real

From the darkness
lead me to light

From death
lead me to immortality.

Map

The globe on the right shows the location of the map below.

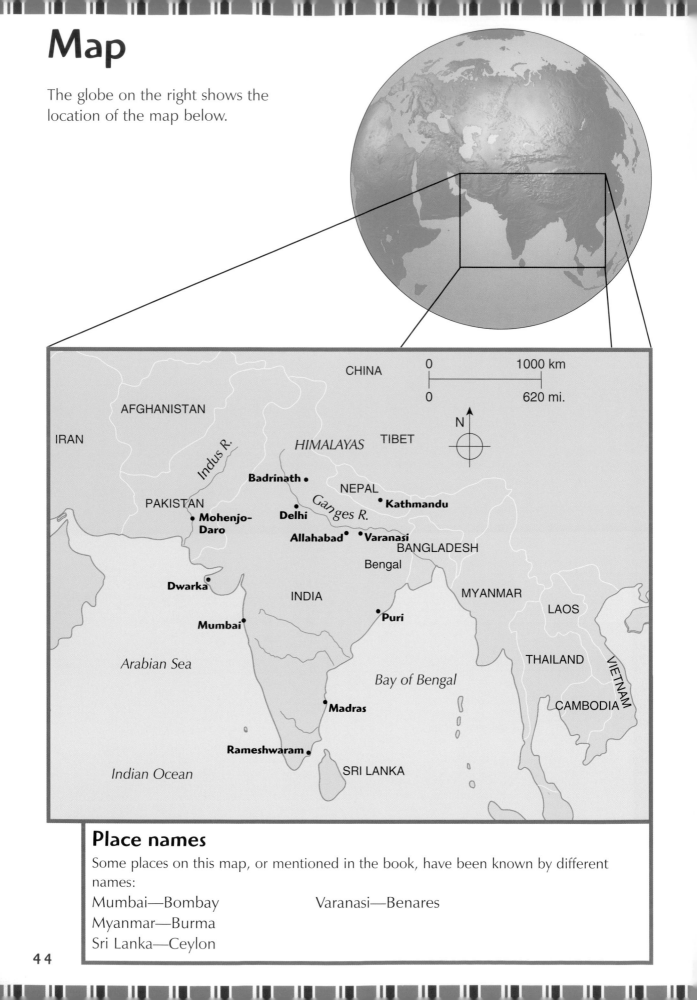

Place names

Some places on this map, or mentioned in the book, have been known by different names:

Mumbai—Bombay   Varanasi—Benares
Myanmar—Burma
Sri Lanka—Ceylon

Timeline

Major events in world history

B.C.E.

3000–1700	Indus Valley Civilization flourished
2500	Pyramids in Egypt built
1800	Stonehenge completed
1000	Nubian Empire (countries around the Nile) – begins and lasts until ca. 350 C.E.
776	First Olympic games
450s	Greece is a center of art and literature under Pericles
336–323	Conquest of Alexander the Great
300	Mayan Civilization begins
200	Great Wall of China begun
48	Julius Caesar becomes Roman emperor
ca. **4**	Jesus of Nazareth born

C.E.

79	Eruption of Vesuvius destroys Pompeii
161–80	"Golden Age" of the Roman Empire under Marcus Aurelius
330	Byzantine Empire begins
868	First printed book (China)
ca.**1000**	Leif Ericson may have discovered America
1300	Ottoman Empire begins (lasts until 1922)
1325	Aztec Empire begins (lasts until 1521)
1400	Black Death kills one person in three throughout China, North Africa, and Europe
1452	Leonardo da Vinci born
1492	Christopher Columbus sails to America
1564	William Shakespeare born
1620	Pilgrims arrive in what is now Massachusetts
1648	Taj Mahal built
1776	U.S. Declaration of Independence
1859	Charles Darwin publishes *The Origin of Species*
1908	Henry Ford produces the first Model-T Ford car
1914–18	World War I
1929	The Wall Street Crash and the Great Depression
1939–45	World War II
1946	First computer invented
1953	Chemical structure of DNA discovered
1969	First Moon landings
1981	AIDS virus diagnosed
1984	Scientists discover a hole in the ozone layer
1989	Berlin Wall torn down
1991	Breakup of the former Soviet Union
1994	Nelson Mandela becomes president of South Africa
2000	Millennium celebrations take place all over the world

Major events in Hindu history

B.C.E.

3000–1700	Indus Valley Civilization and worship of nature gods
1500	**Aryans** invade Indus Valley and introduce worship of cosmic gods
1200	Beginning of the stories of the **Vedas**
400–200	*Upanishads* written down
ca. **300**	*Mahabharata* first written down
273–232	Life of **Buddhist** Emperor Ashoka and decline of Hinduism
ca. **100**	The *Ramayana* first written down

C.E.

300	Laws of Manu written down
230–480	Gupta Empire (settled time for Hinduism)
500	**Puranas** first written down
788–820	Life of Shankara (developed important Hindu teachings)
999–1030	Life of Mahmud of Ghazni (first **Muslim** ruler in India)
1100	Life of Ramanuja (important Hindu teacher and leader)
1100–1500	Islamic Mughals invade India three times, many Hindu temples destroyed
1173–1206	Life of Muhammad of Ghur (second Muslim ruler in India)
1400	Vedas written down
1526–1707	Mughal (Islamic) Empire rules India
1834–1886	Life of Ramakrishna (holy man and leader)
1863–1902	Vivekananda (promoted Hinduism as a world religion)
1869–1948	Life of Mahatma Gandhi, religious and political leader
1947	Indian independence from Great Britain

Glossary

ahimsa	nonviolence and respect for life
artha	providing for your family, the second goal in life
arti	worship of Brahman through fire
Aryans	ancient people believed to have lived between central Asia and eastern Europe in the second century B.C.E.
ashrama	one of the four stages of life
Atman	soul that is in everything
Aum	sacred sound and symbol for Hindus
avatar	appearance of a god, especially the god Vishnu
bhajan	religious song used in worship
Brahman	Hindu name for the Great Power; highest of the four varnas
Buddhist	follower of Buddha Gautama
caste	one of four hereditary social groups that determine a person's position in society
cremation	burning of a dead body
darshan	"see"—the moment of contact between Brahman and worshiper
dharma	"duty"—the first goal in life for Hindus
discrimination	ill-treatment because of race or religion
diva	small clay lamp used at the festival of Diwali
eternal	lasting forever
fast	in Hinduism, to go without certain foods for religious reasons
funeral pyre	fire used for cremation
ghat	platform by a river used for worship or burning a dead body
ghee	melted butter that is completely free of any solids, so that it is clear
Gujarati	language of the northwestern region of India
guru	Hindu holy man or religious teacher
harijan	"children of God"—lowest group in traditional Indian society, formerly called "untouchables"
henna	reddish-brown dye that comes from a plant
horoscope	way of telling the future, based on the position of the stars
hymn	religious song
jati	smaller group within a hereditary social class that formerly determined a person's profession
kama	regulated sense of enjoyment, the third goal in life
karma	"action"—the actions of this life that affect future lives
Kshatriya	one of four hereditary social groups; rulers and warriors
linga	stone columns that are a symbol of Shiva
mandir	Gujarati name for a Hindu place of worship

mantra	repeated prayer, often a verse from Hindu holy books
meditation	training the mind to concentrate in a particular way
moksha	freedom from the cycle of rebirth
monsoon	season of very heavy rainfall in India
murti	image of a god or goddess
Muslim	follower of the religion of Islam
pandit	priest who leads worship and offers advice to people
pilgrimage	journey for religious reasons
prashad	food that has been blessed by a god and that is given at the end of Hindu worship
puja	worship
pujari	priest who leads worship in a temple
Puranas	part of the Hindu holy books; long story in verse that contain Hindu myths and stories about Hindu gods, goddesses, and heroes
reincarnation	belief that the soul never dies but is reborn into another life
Rig-Veda	oldest of Hindu holy writings that were passed on by word of mouth for centuries before being written down
samsara	continual cycle of death and rebirth
samskars	sixteen ceremonies to mark the stages of life
Sanatan dharma	eternal truths; name for Hinduism
Sanskrit	ancient written Indian language
sari	length of fabric worn as a dress
scriptures	holy writings
shrine	holy place often set aside for worship
shroud	large piece of cloth used to wrap a dead body
shruti	"heard"—name for some of the Hindu holy books containing words that were passed down by word of mouth before they were written down
Sudras	lowest of the four varnas
sin	wrongdoing
smriti	"remembered"—name for some of the Hindu holy books
symbol	expressing something important without using words
tilak	powder mark placed on the forehead to show that a Hindu has been to worship
Upanishad	mystical and philosophical dialogue that is part of the oldest of the Hindu holy books
Vaishyas	one of four hereditary social groups; merchants and professionals
varna	a group of society; in the caste system, people are divided into four varnas
Vedas	oldest of the Hindu holy books
yoga	path—way to achieve freedom from the cycle of death and rebirth

More Books to Read

Ganeri, Anita. *Hindu*. Danbury, Conn.: Children's Press, 1996.

Kadodwala, Dilip. *Hindu Festivals*. Chicago: Heinemann Library, 1997.

Index